Coloring book for adults and kids amazing lamb design

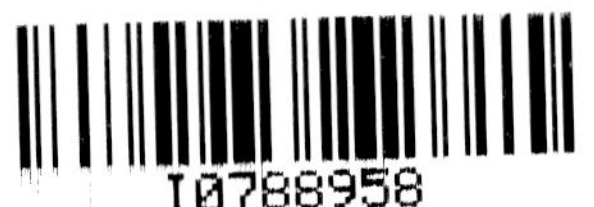

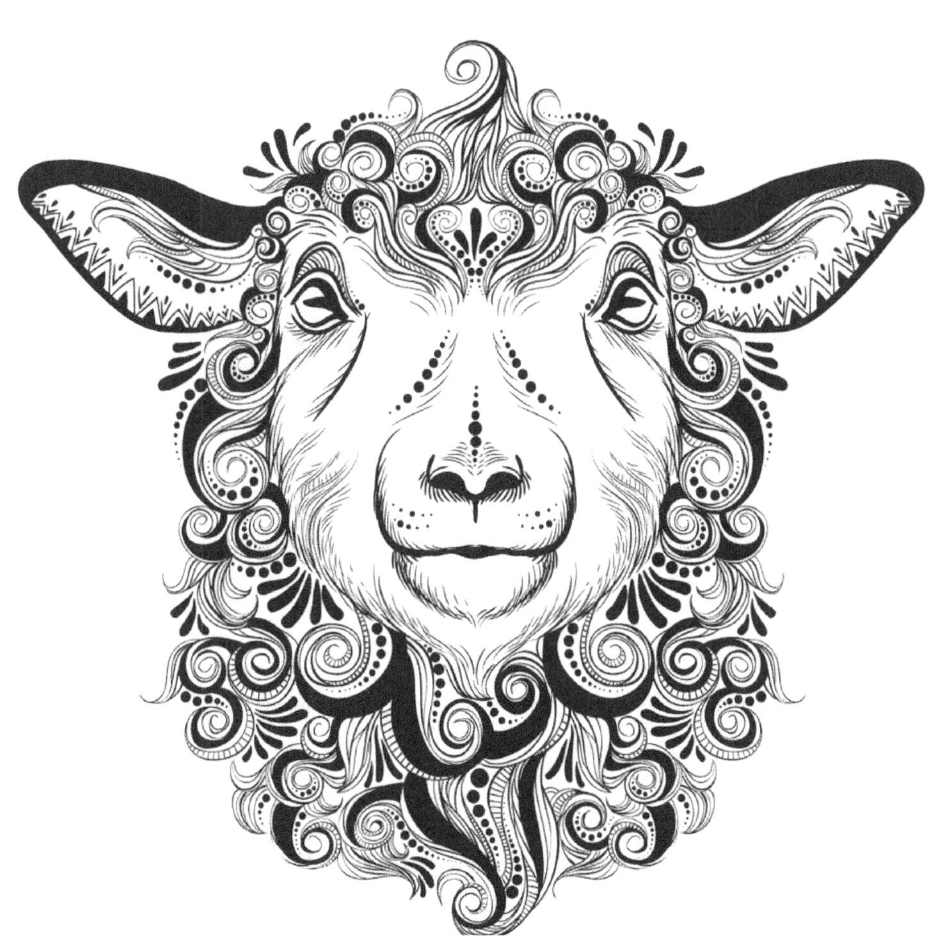

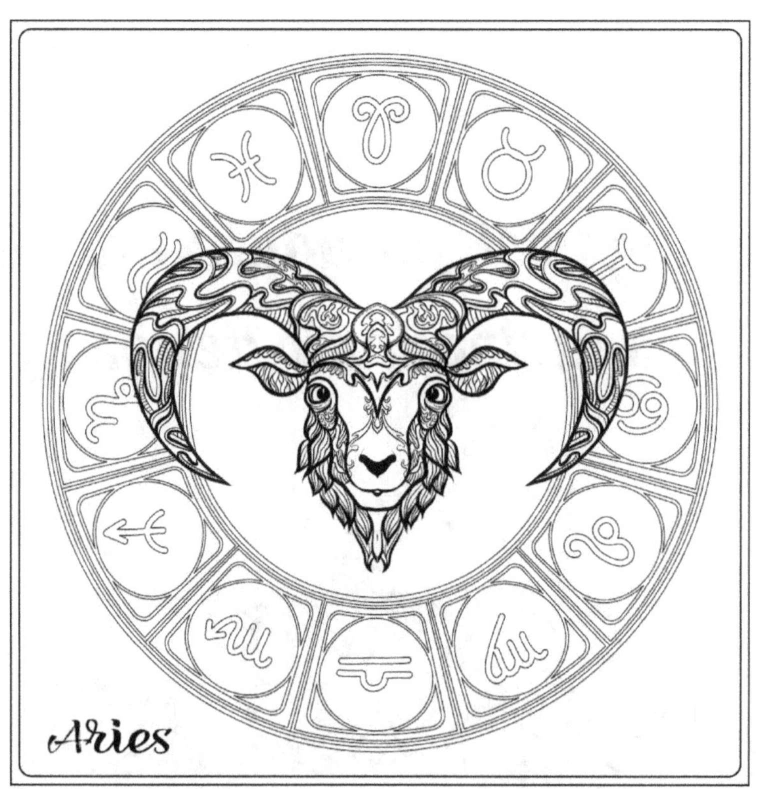

This coloring book is belongs to

____

____

____

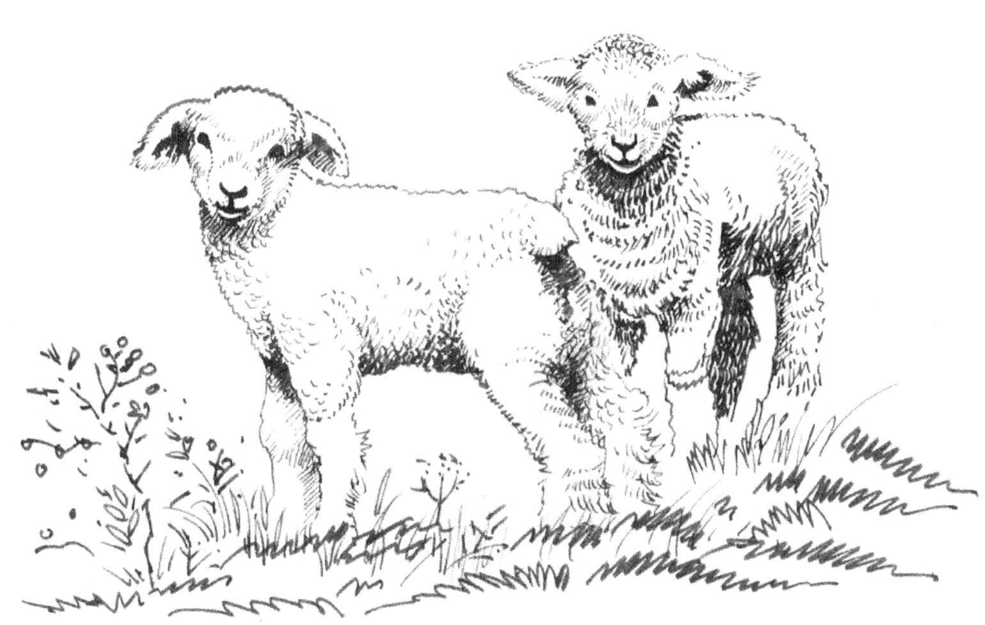

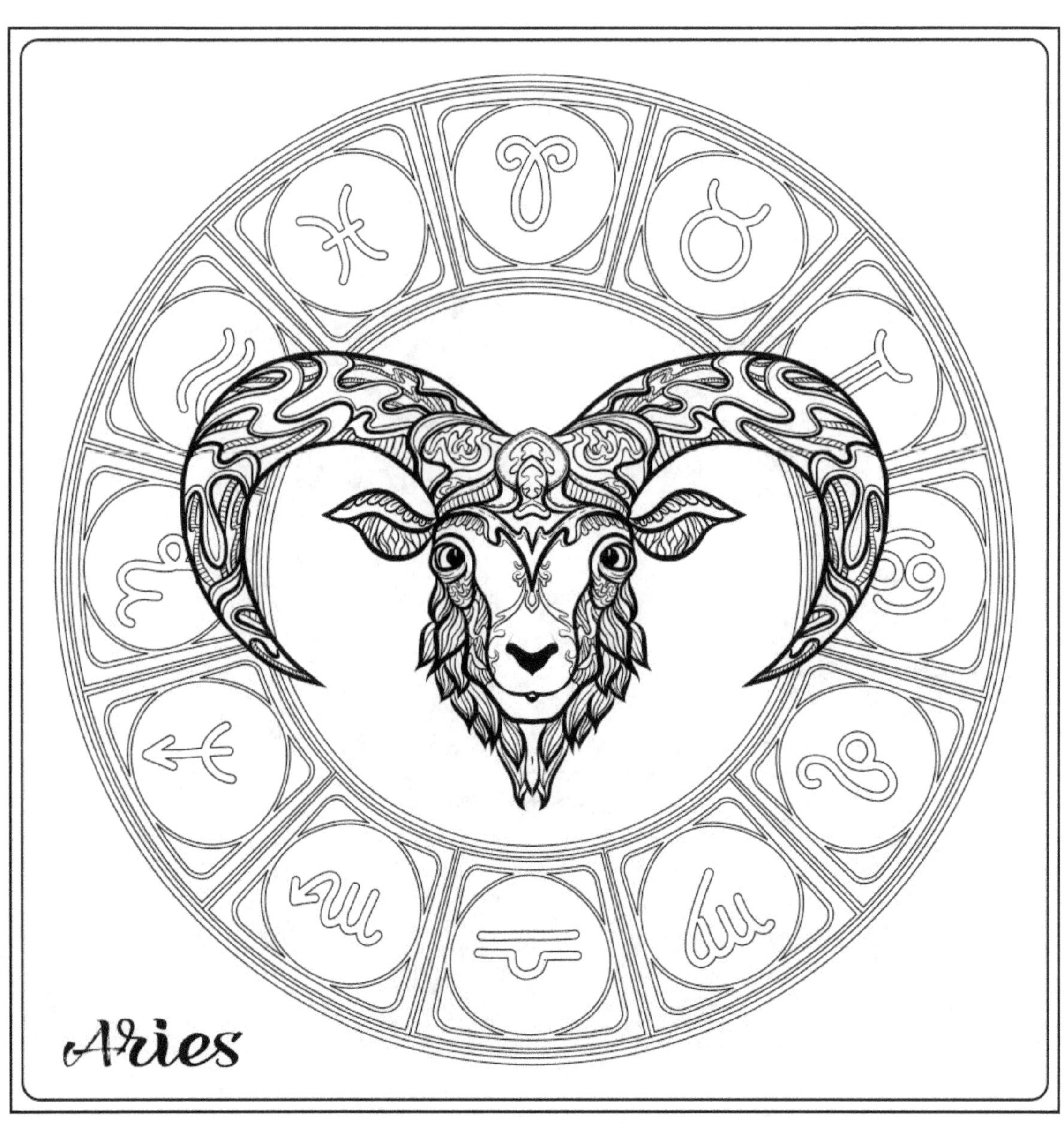

Aries

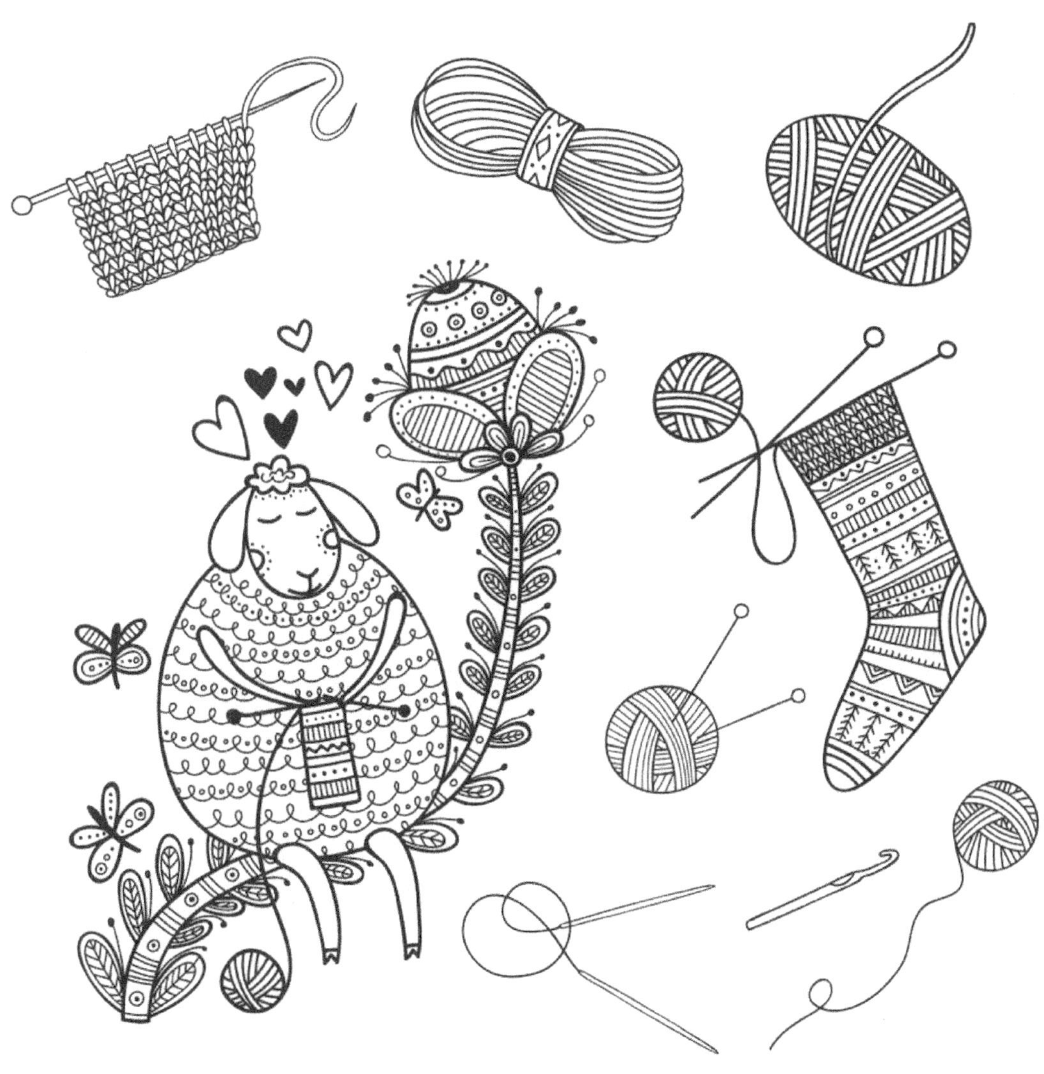

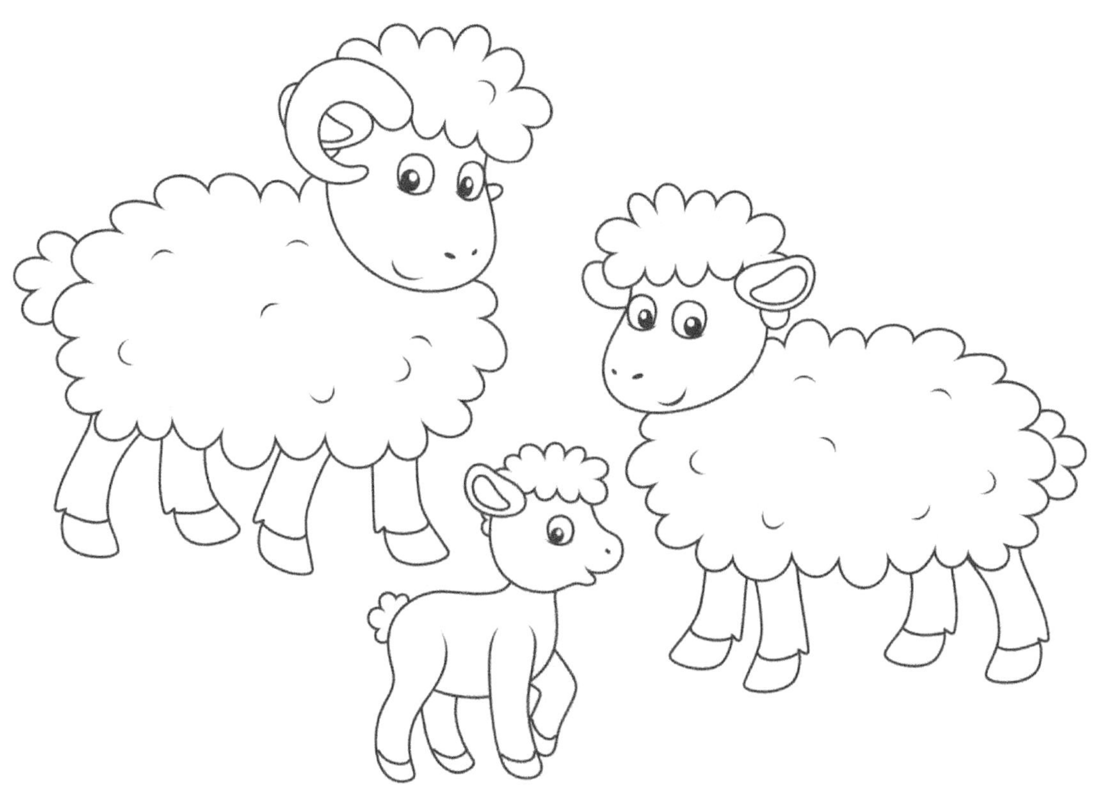

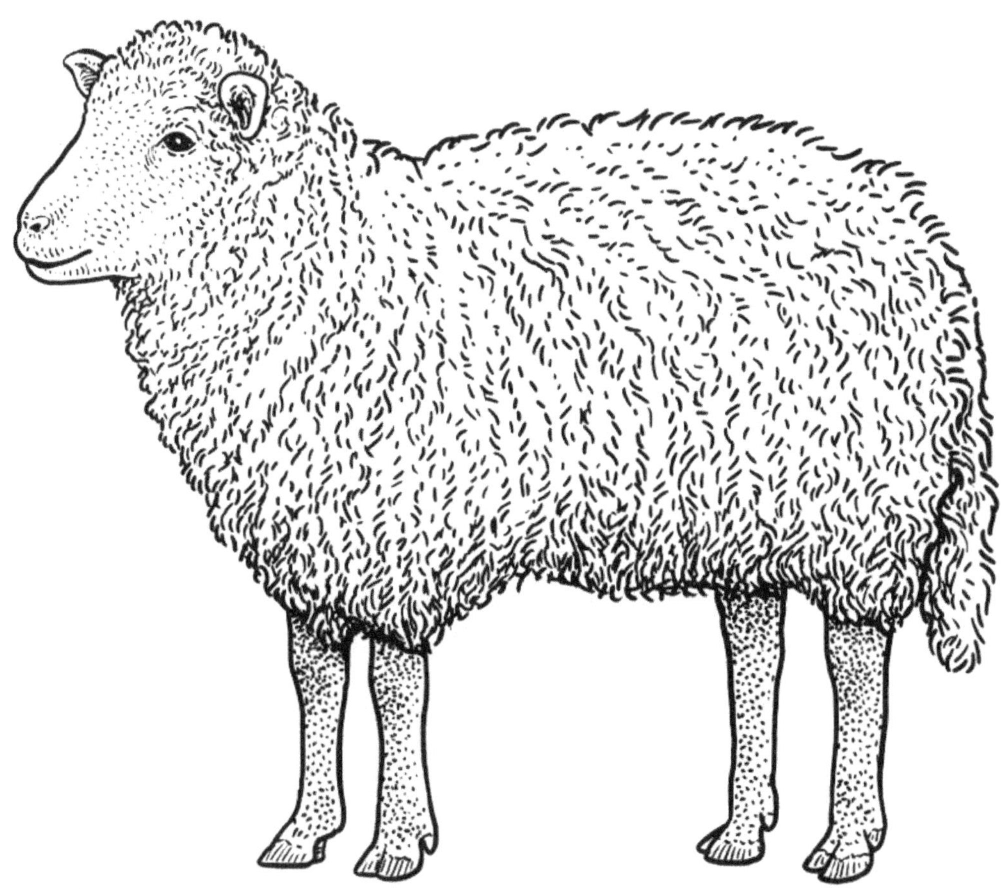

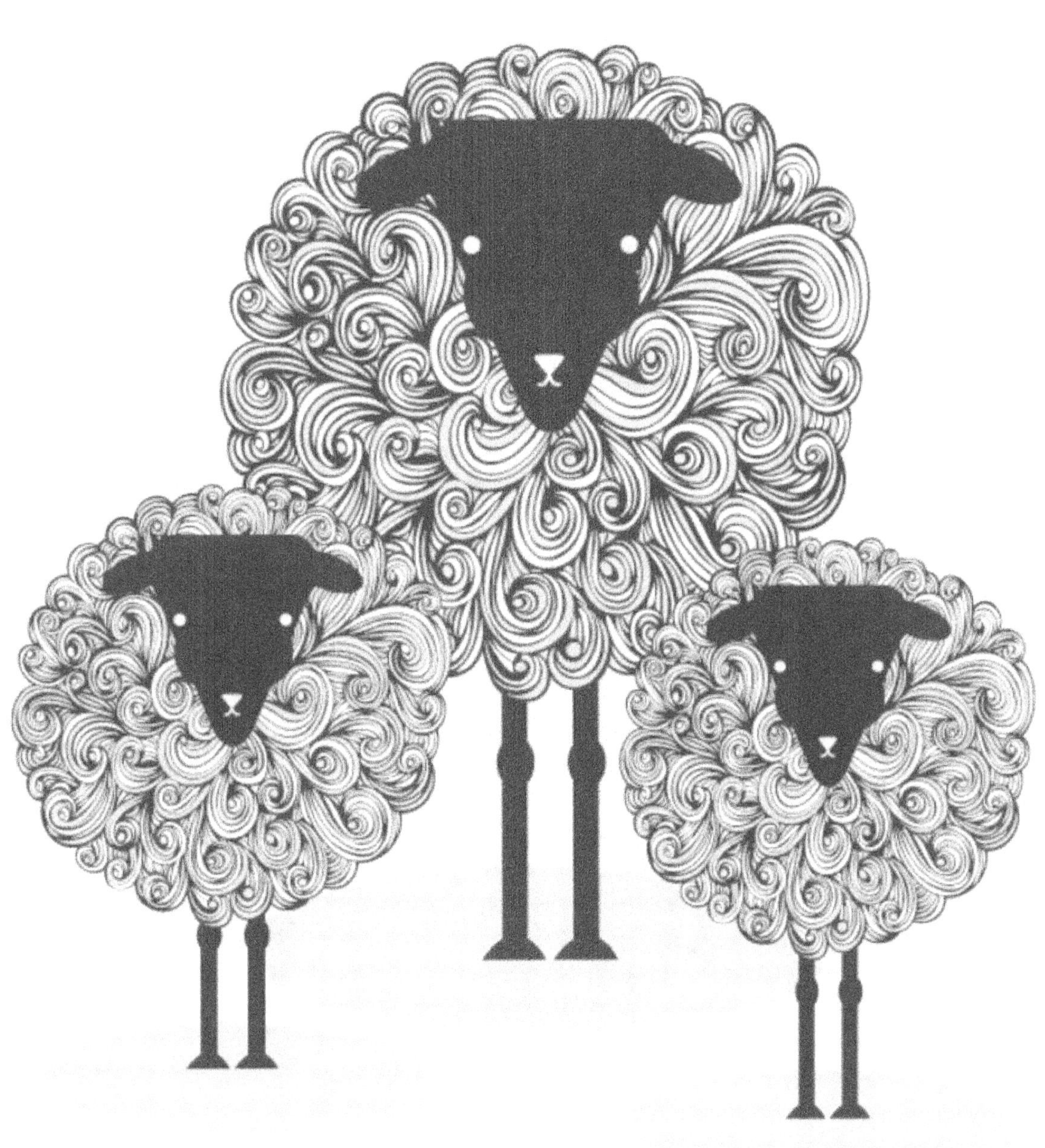

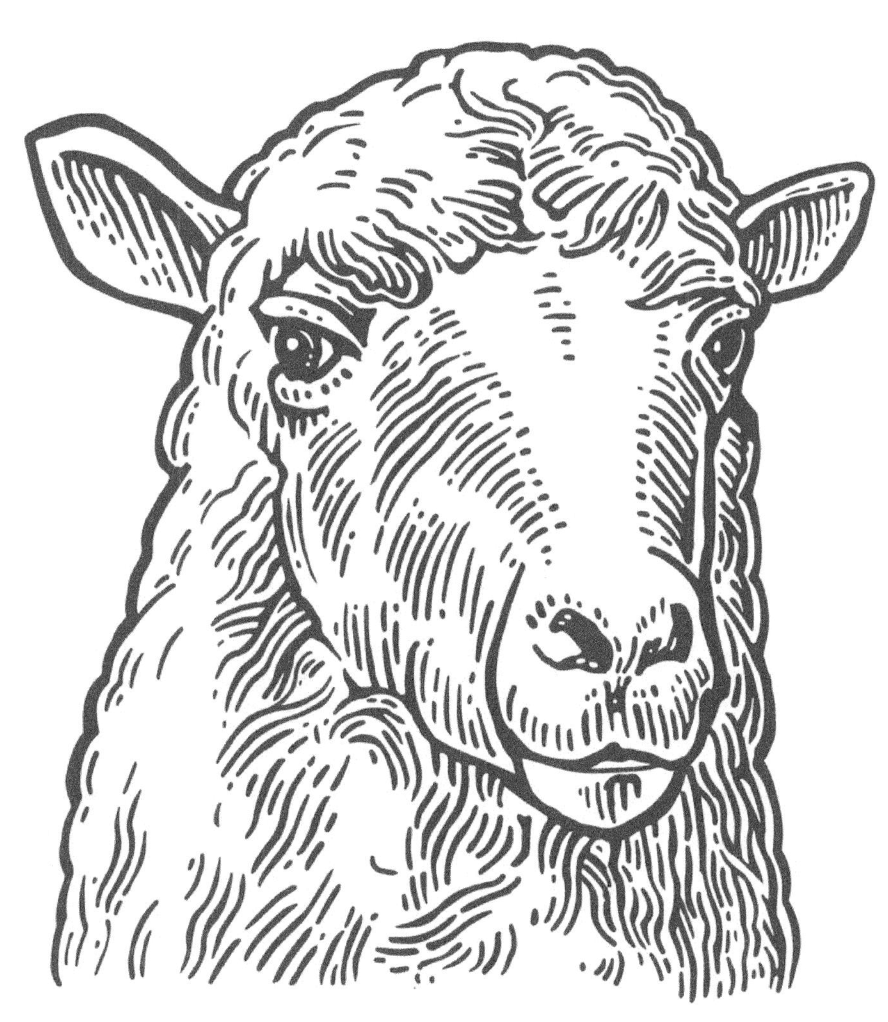

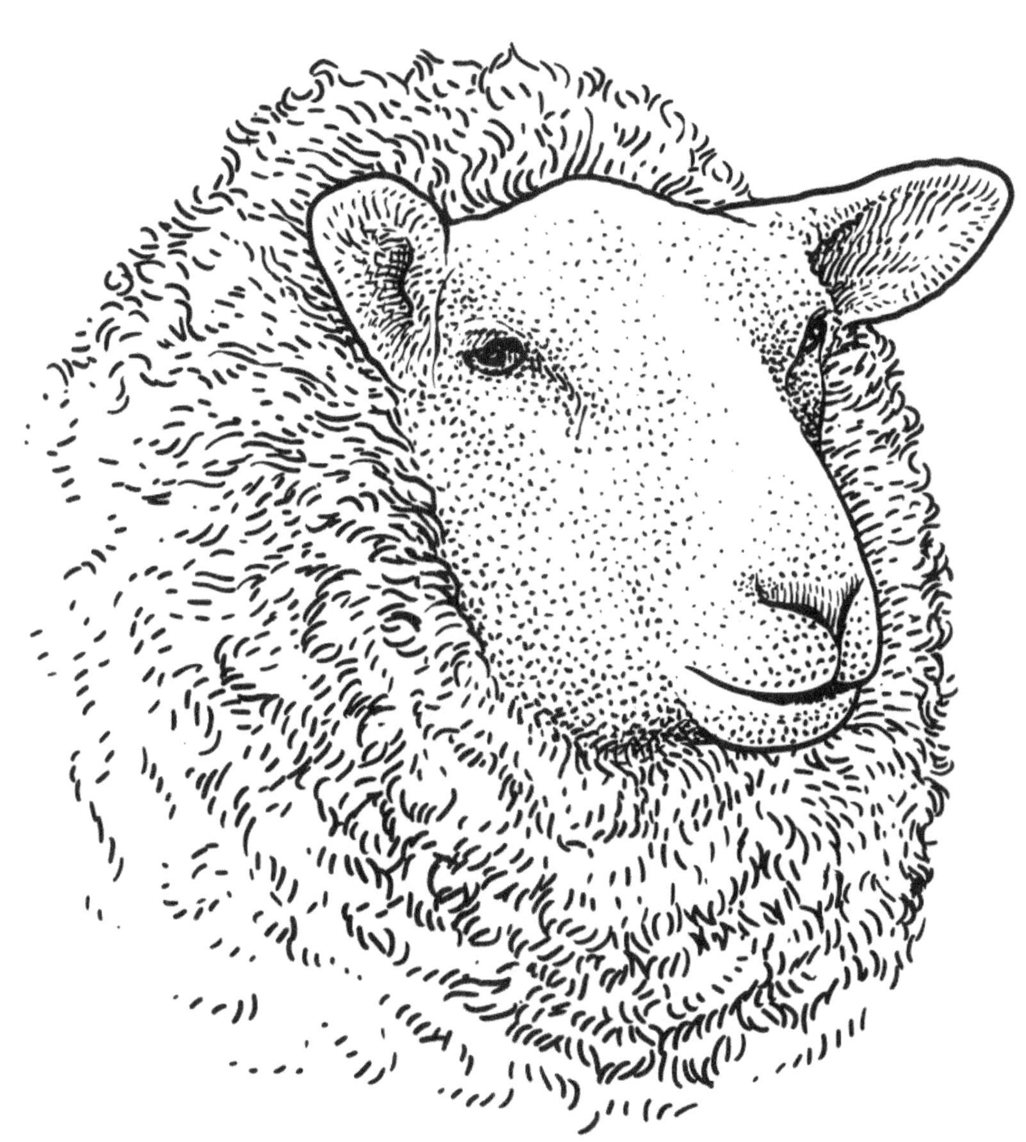

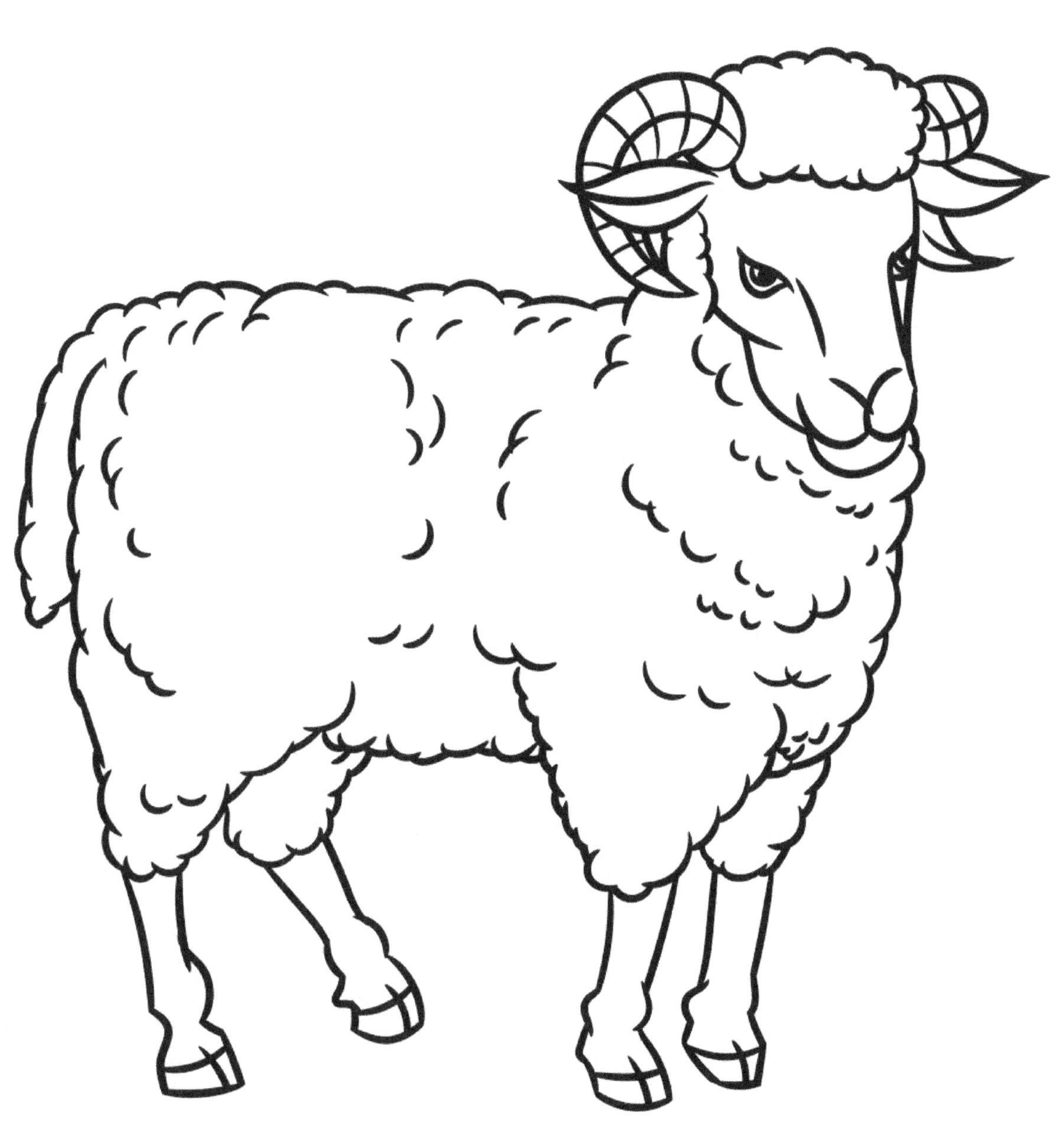

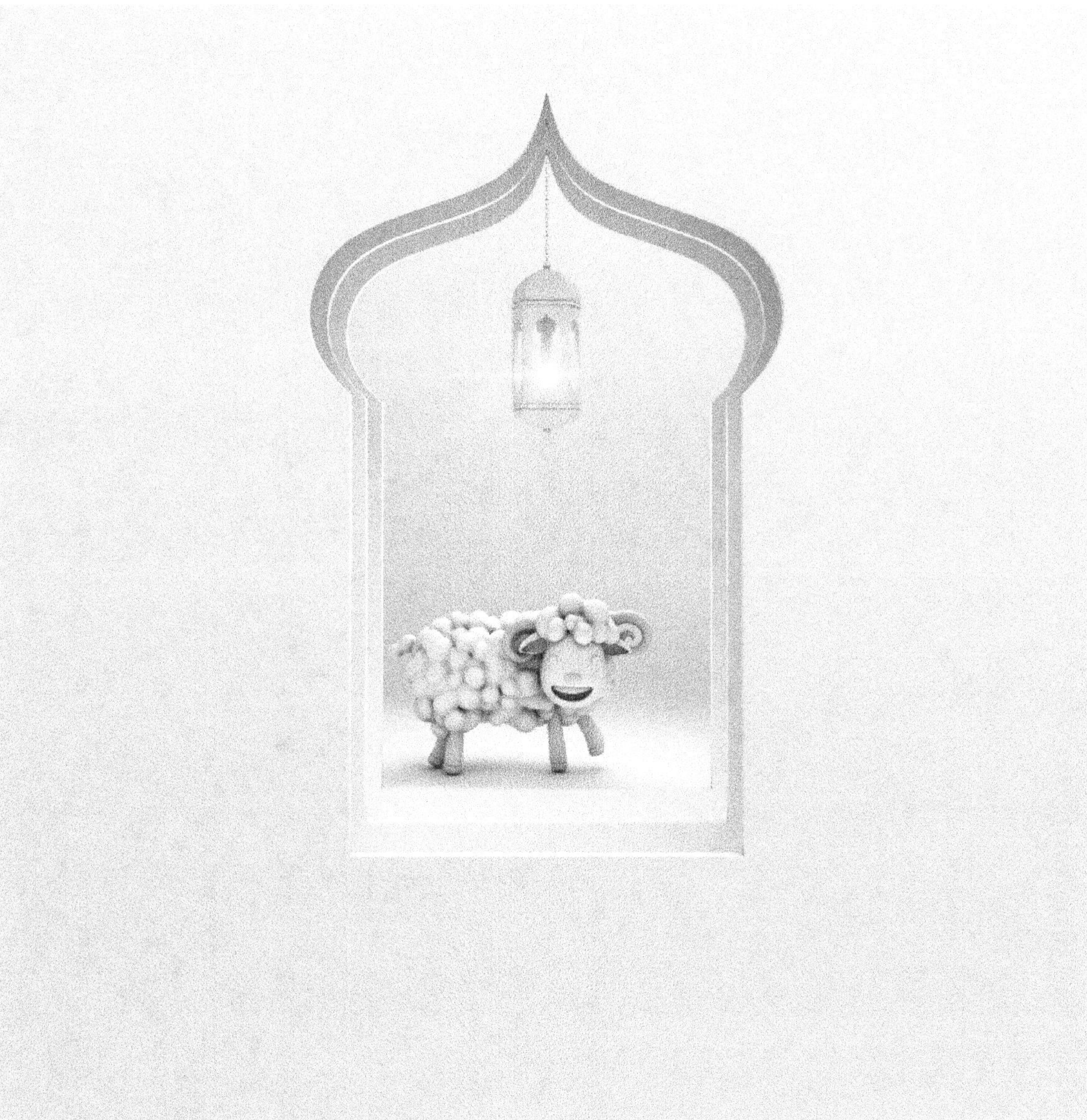

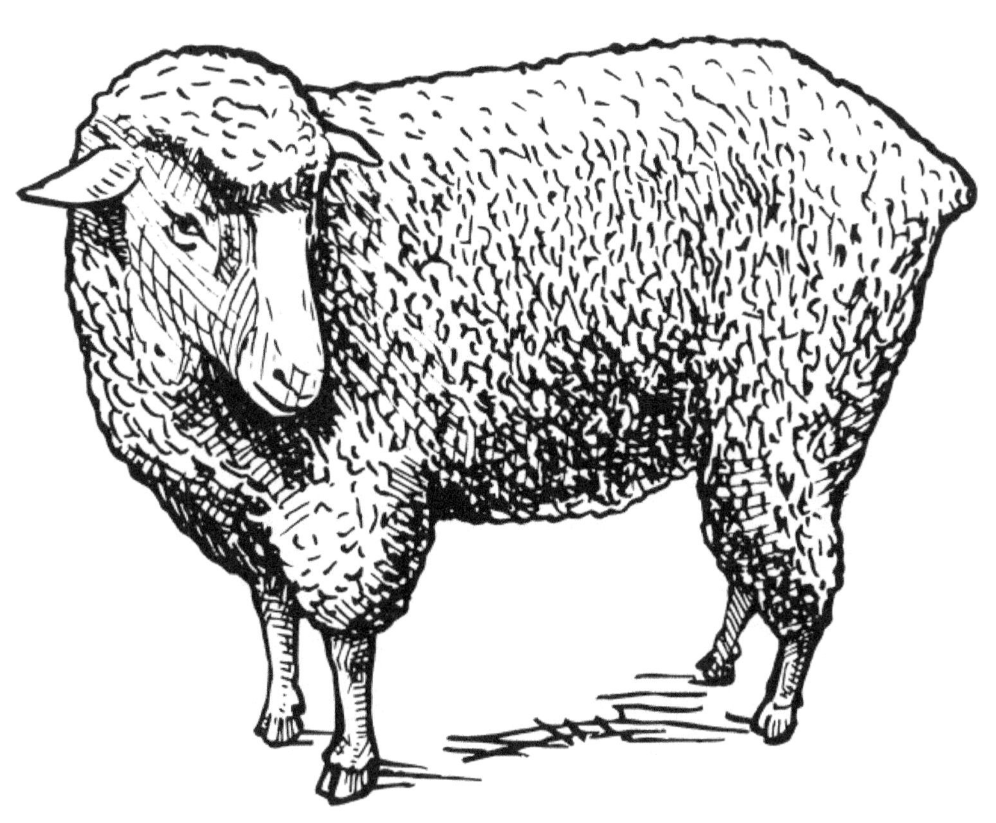

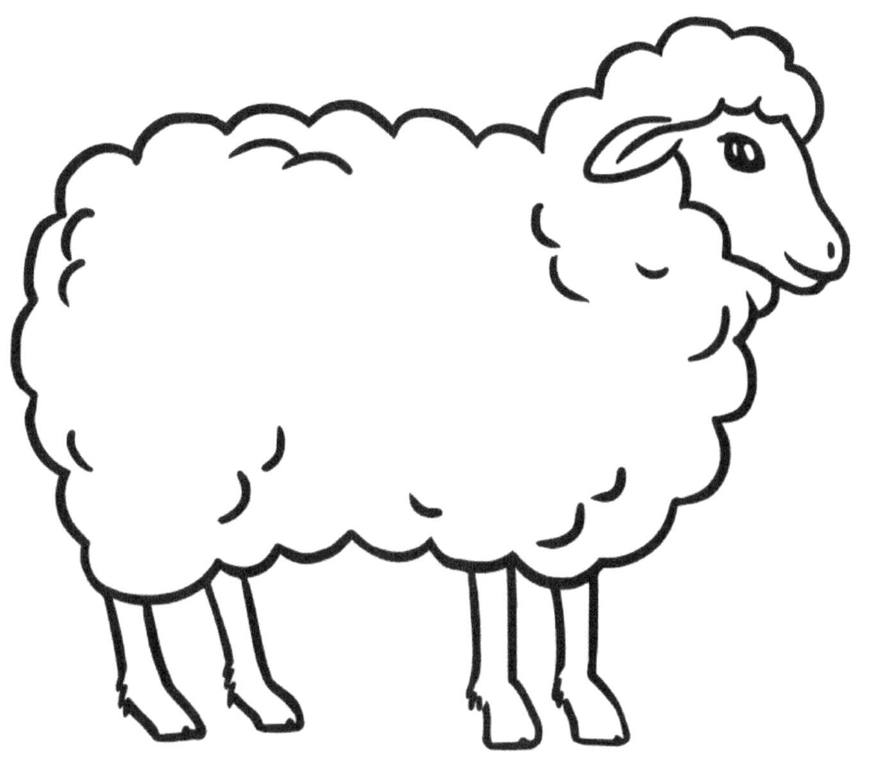

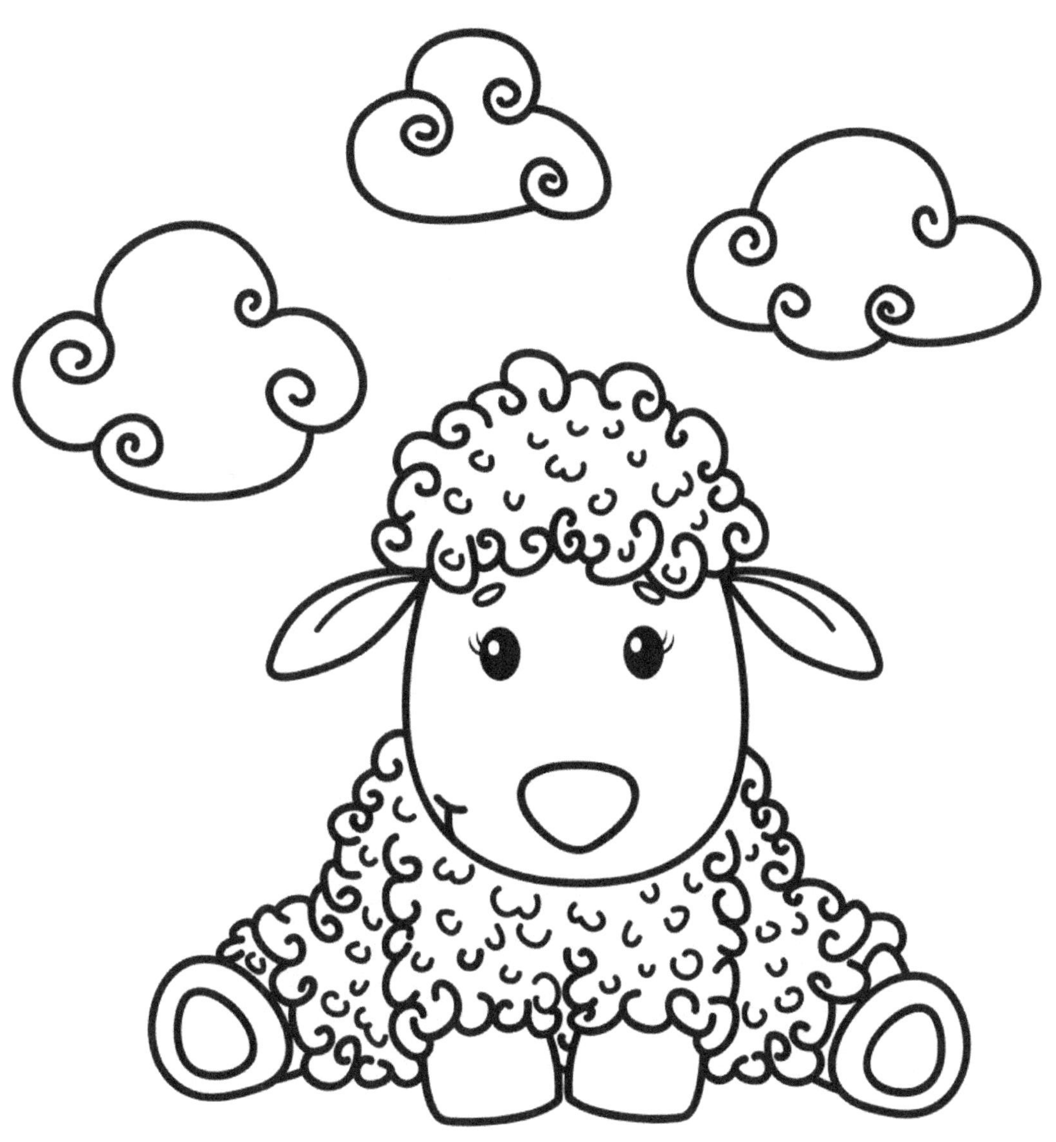

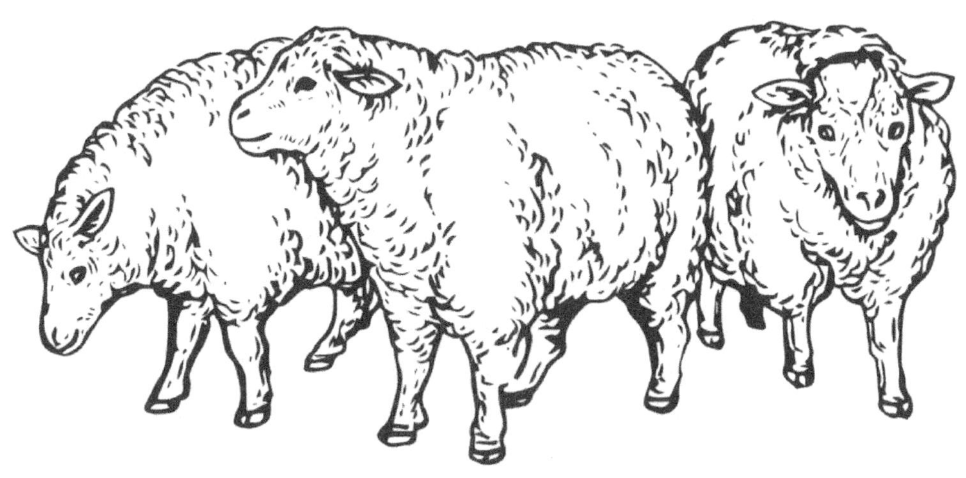

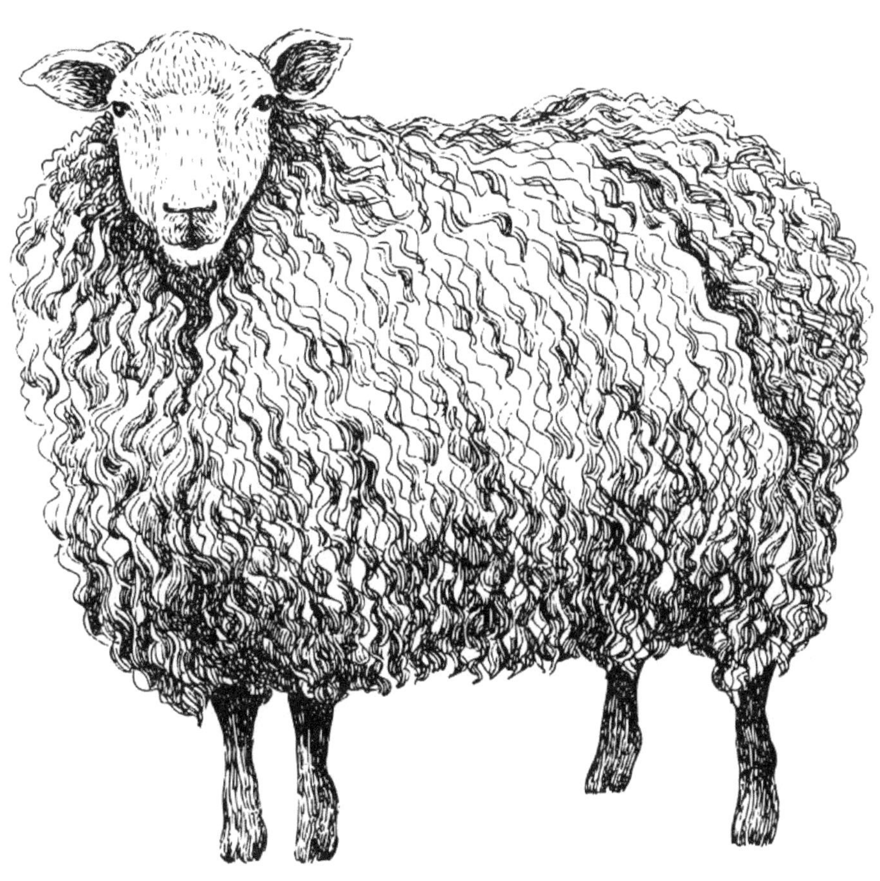

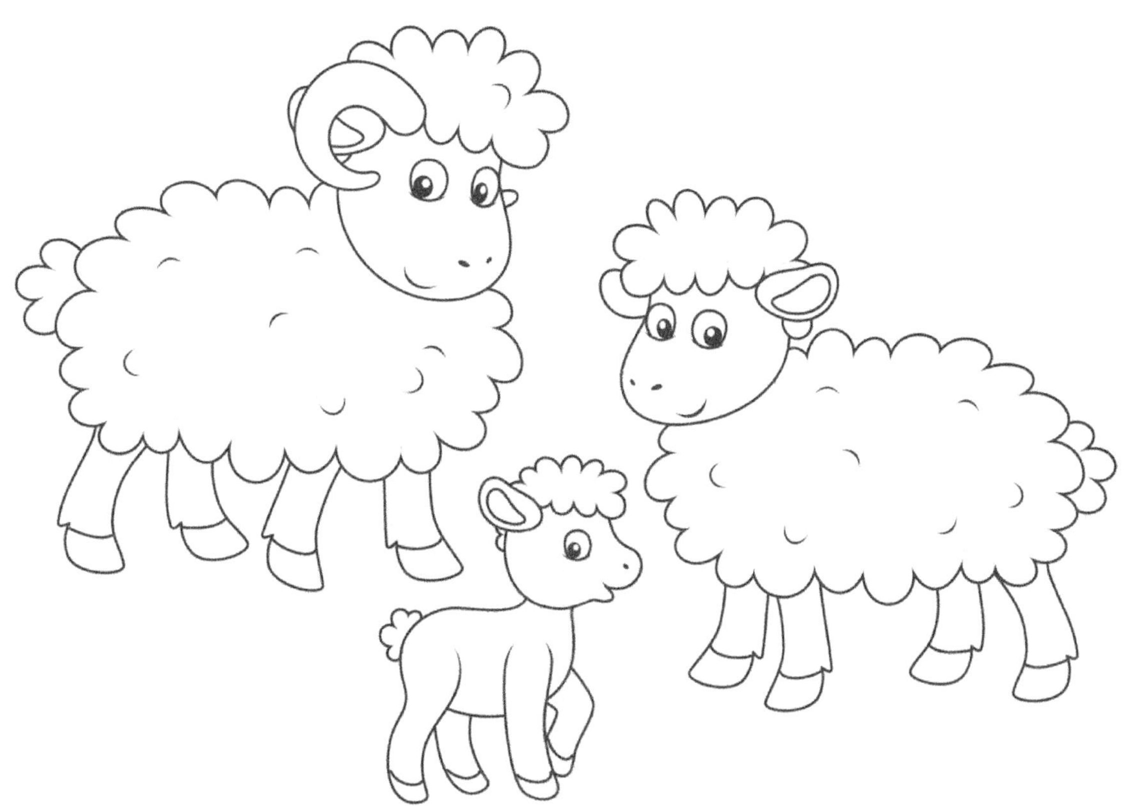

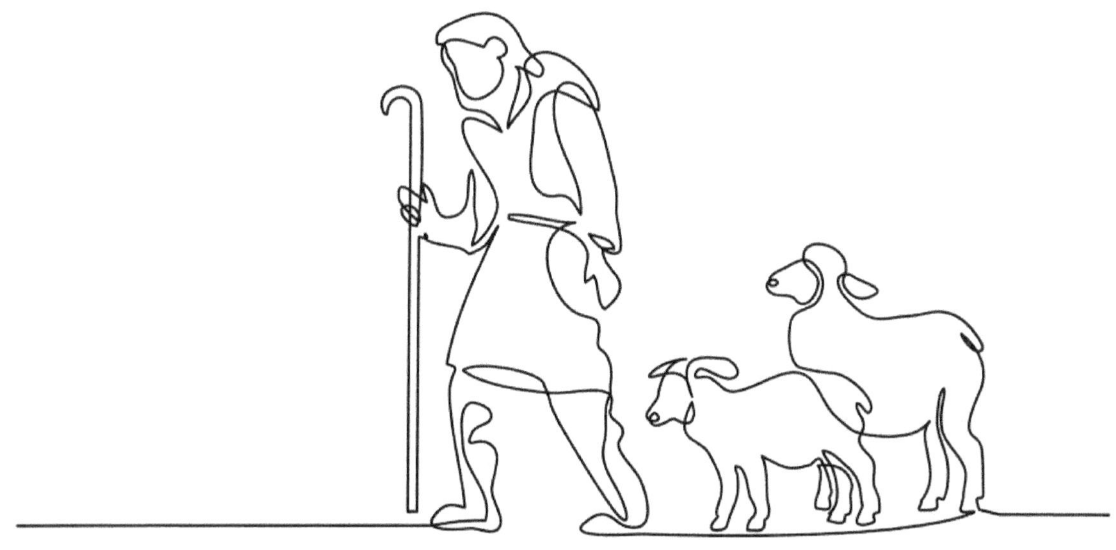

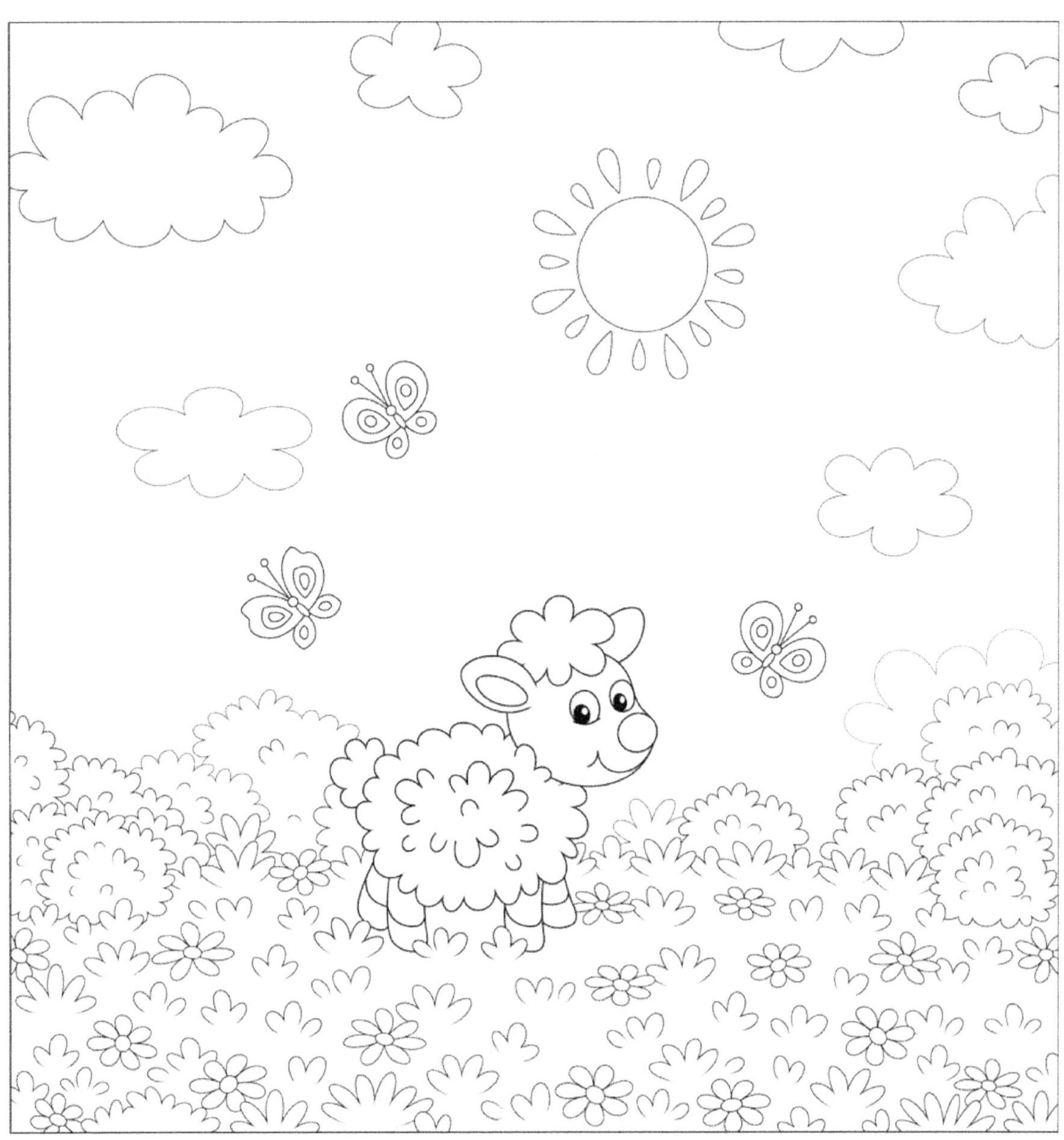

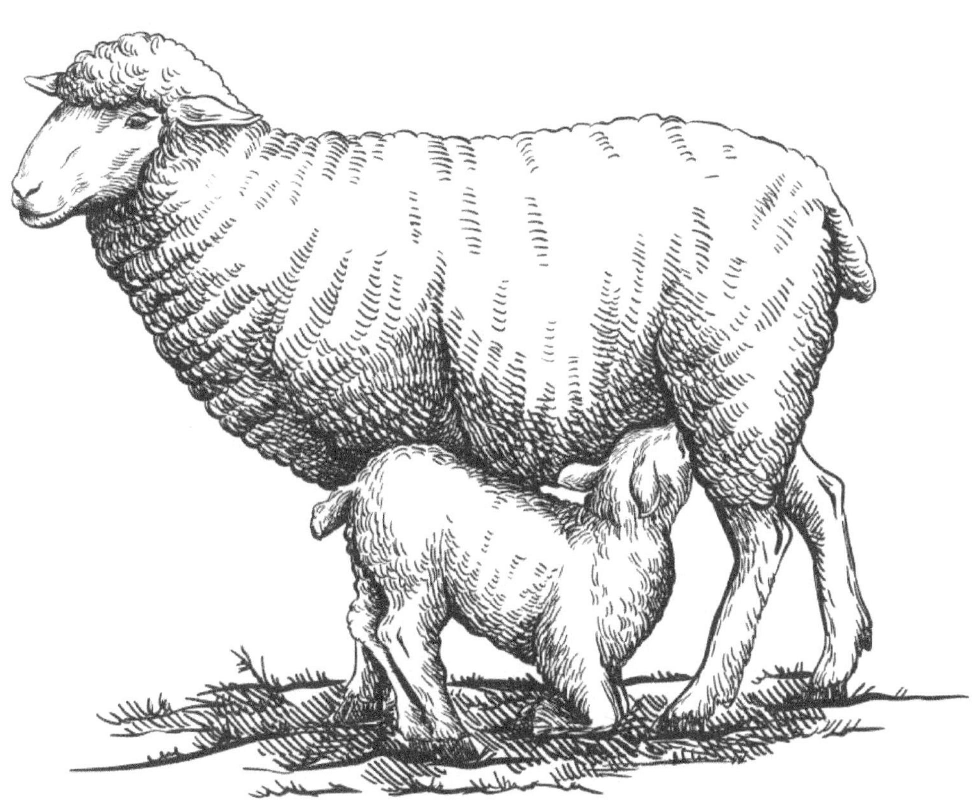

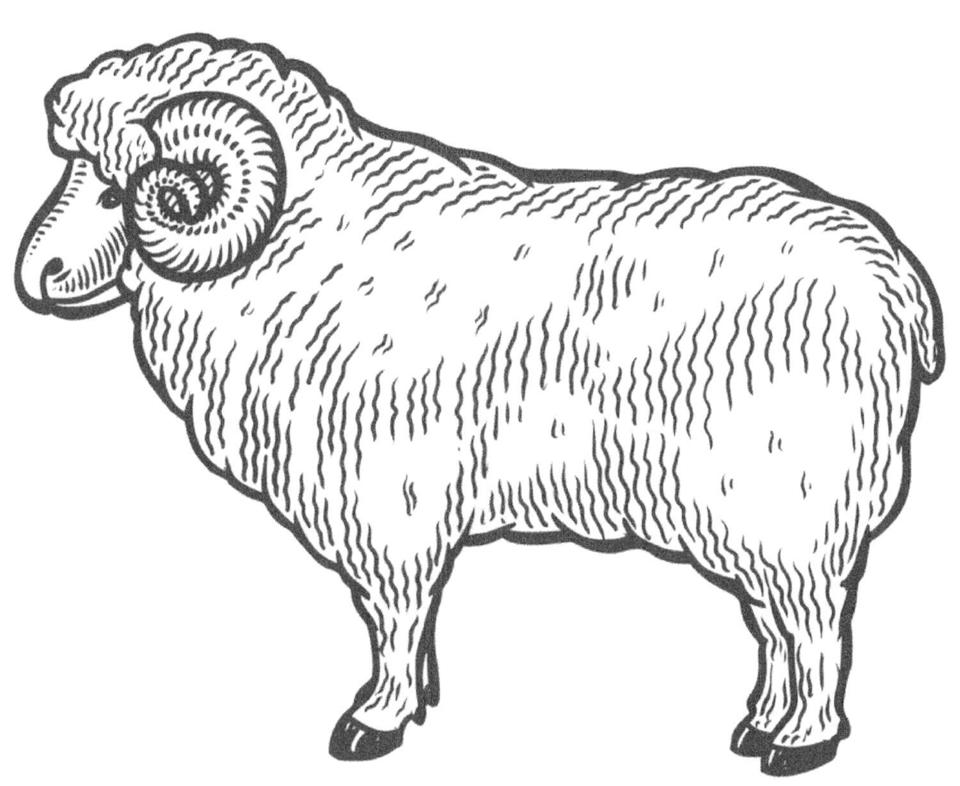

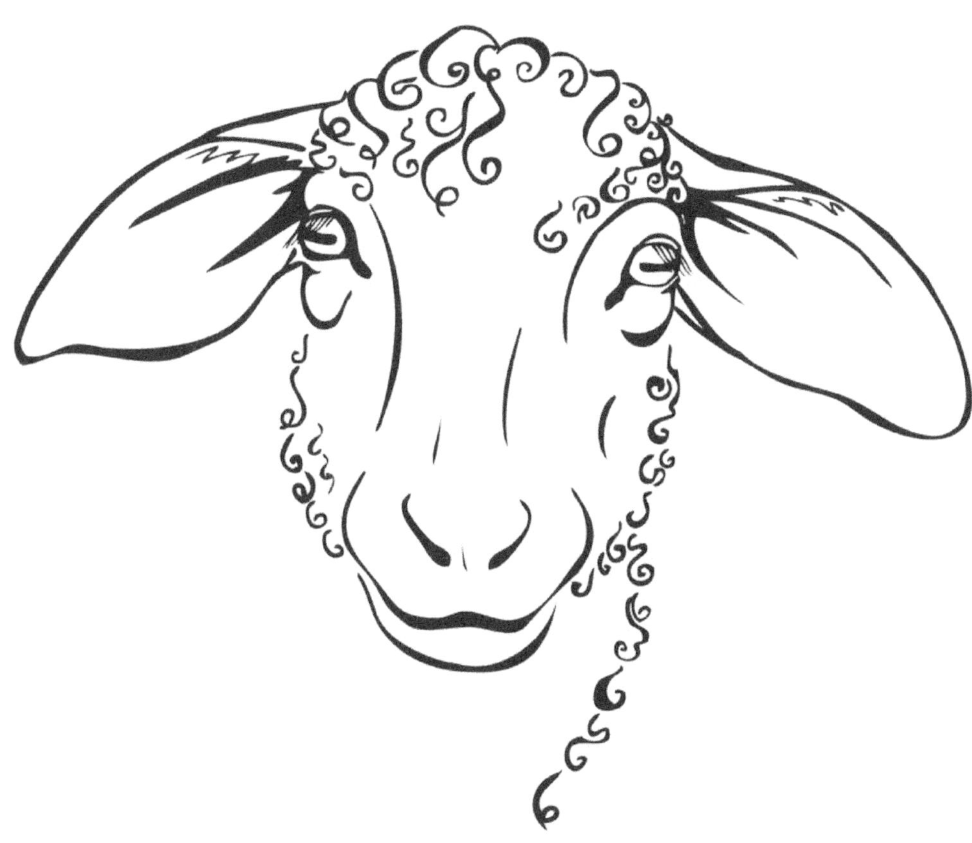

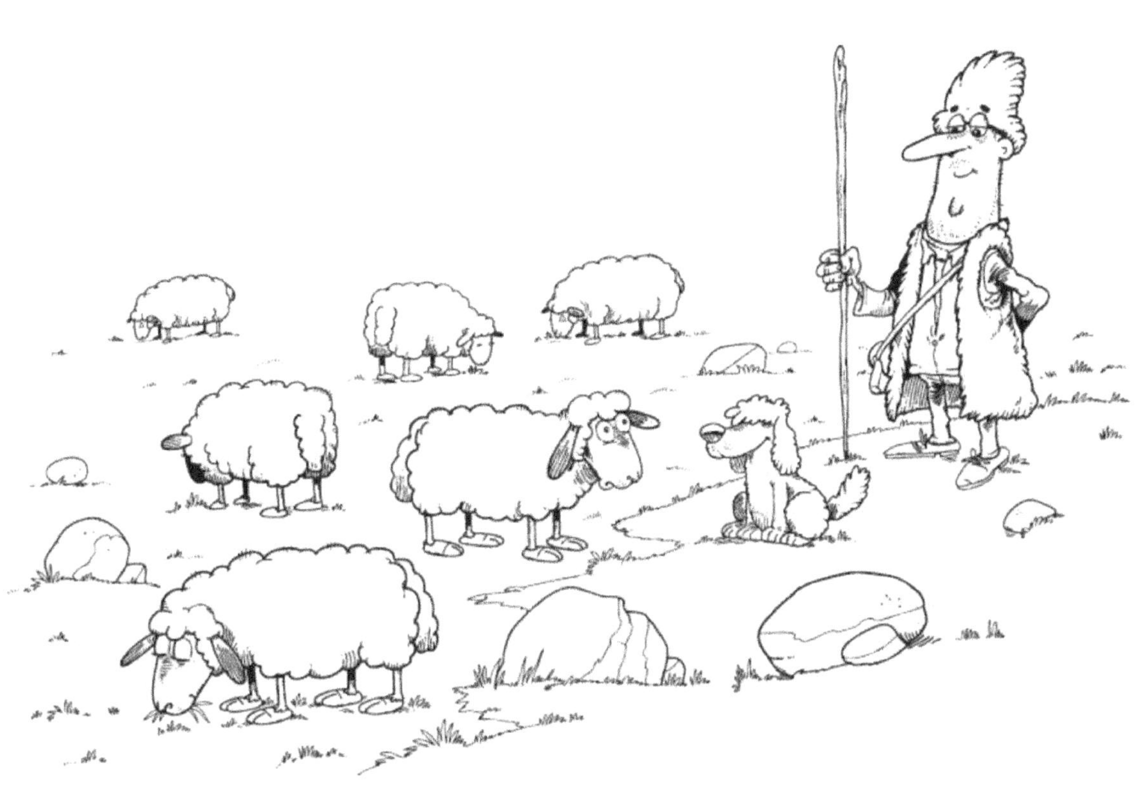

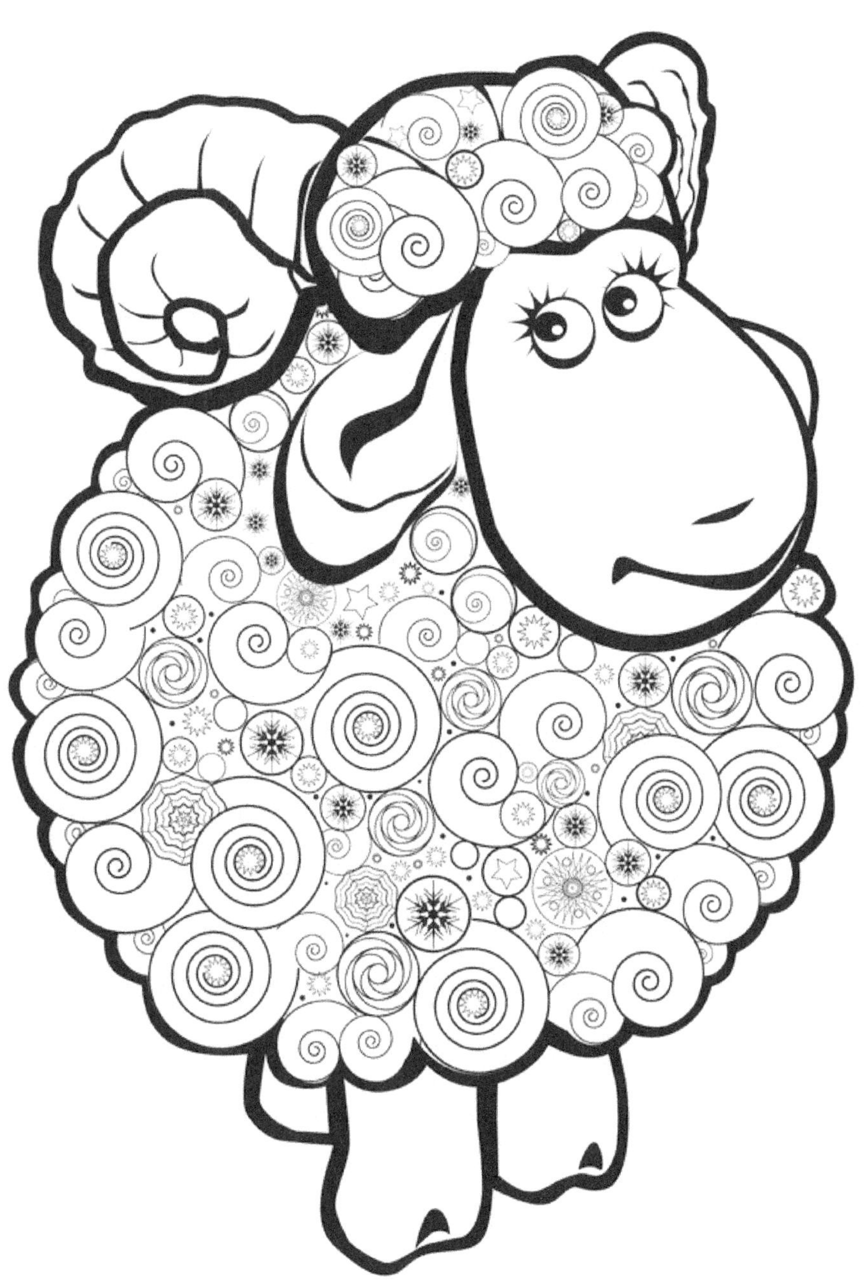

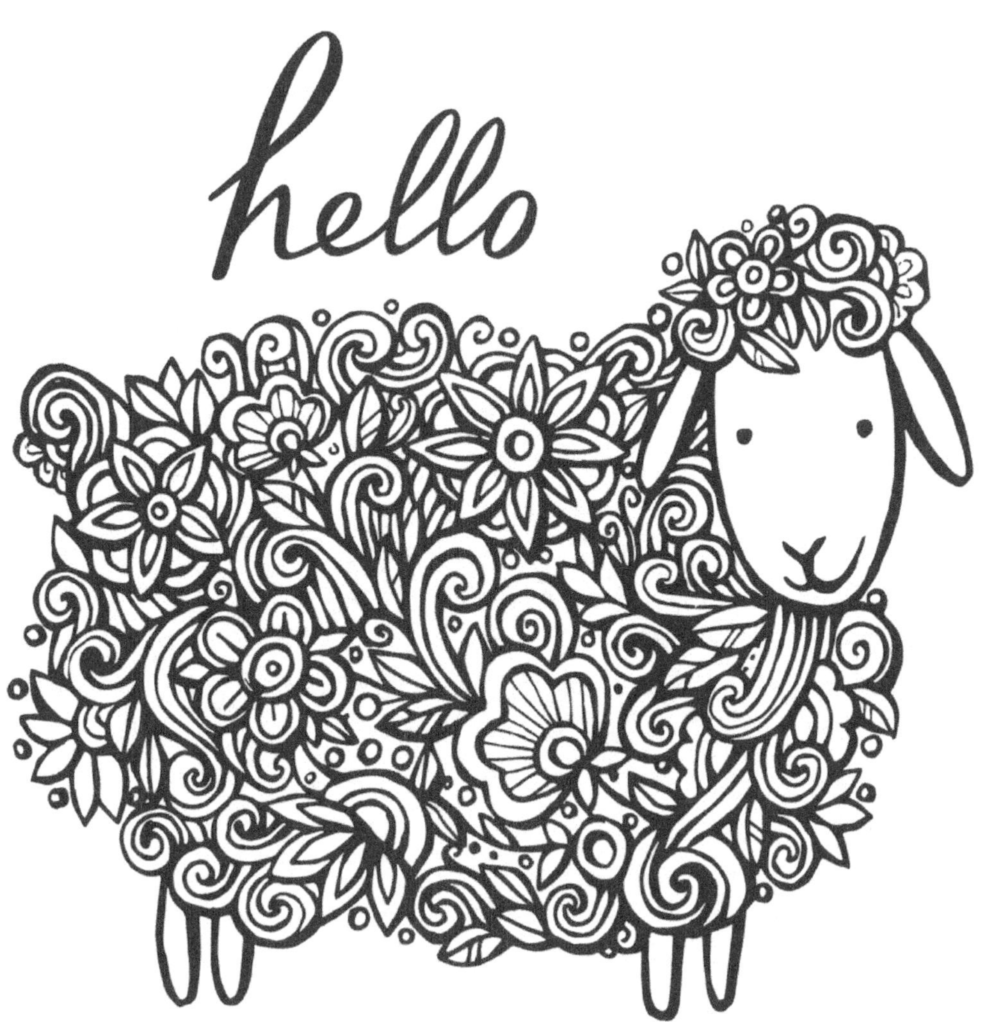
hello

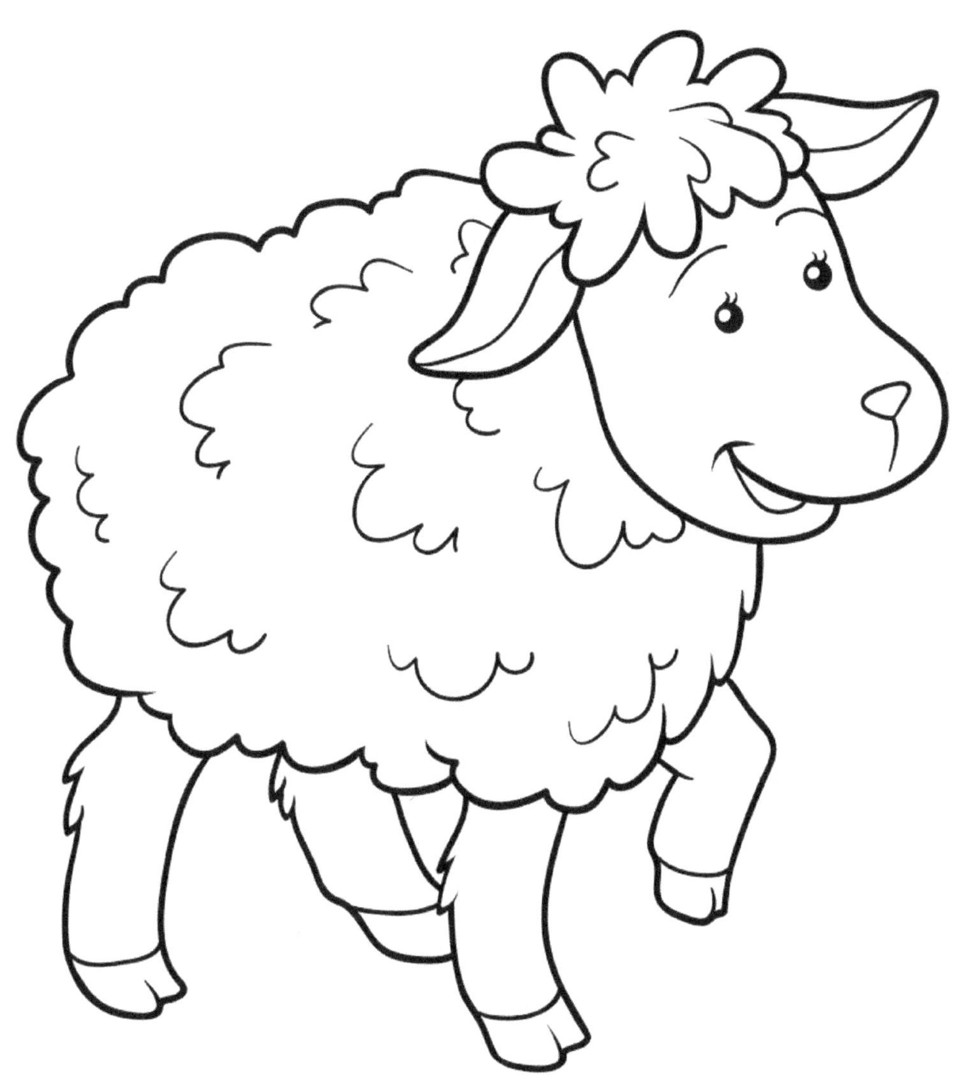

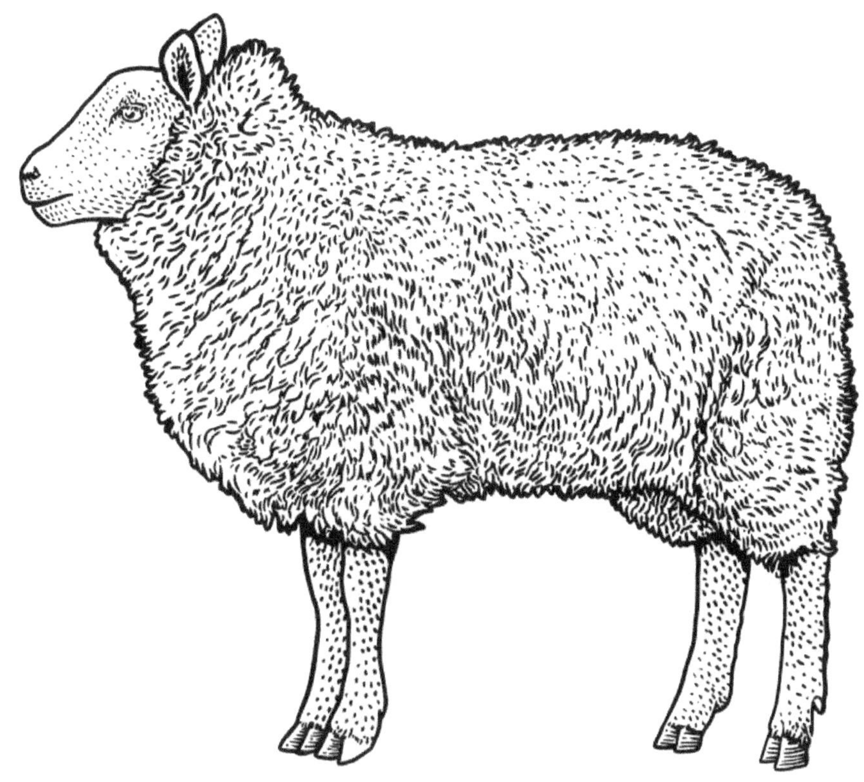

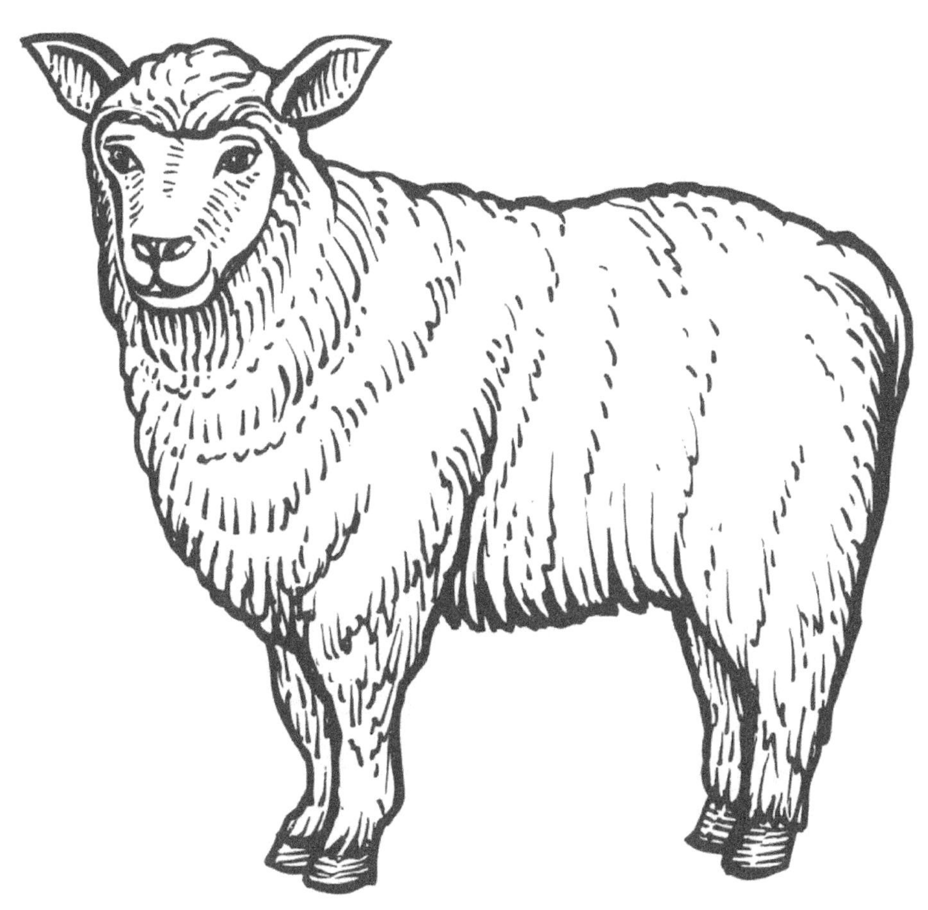

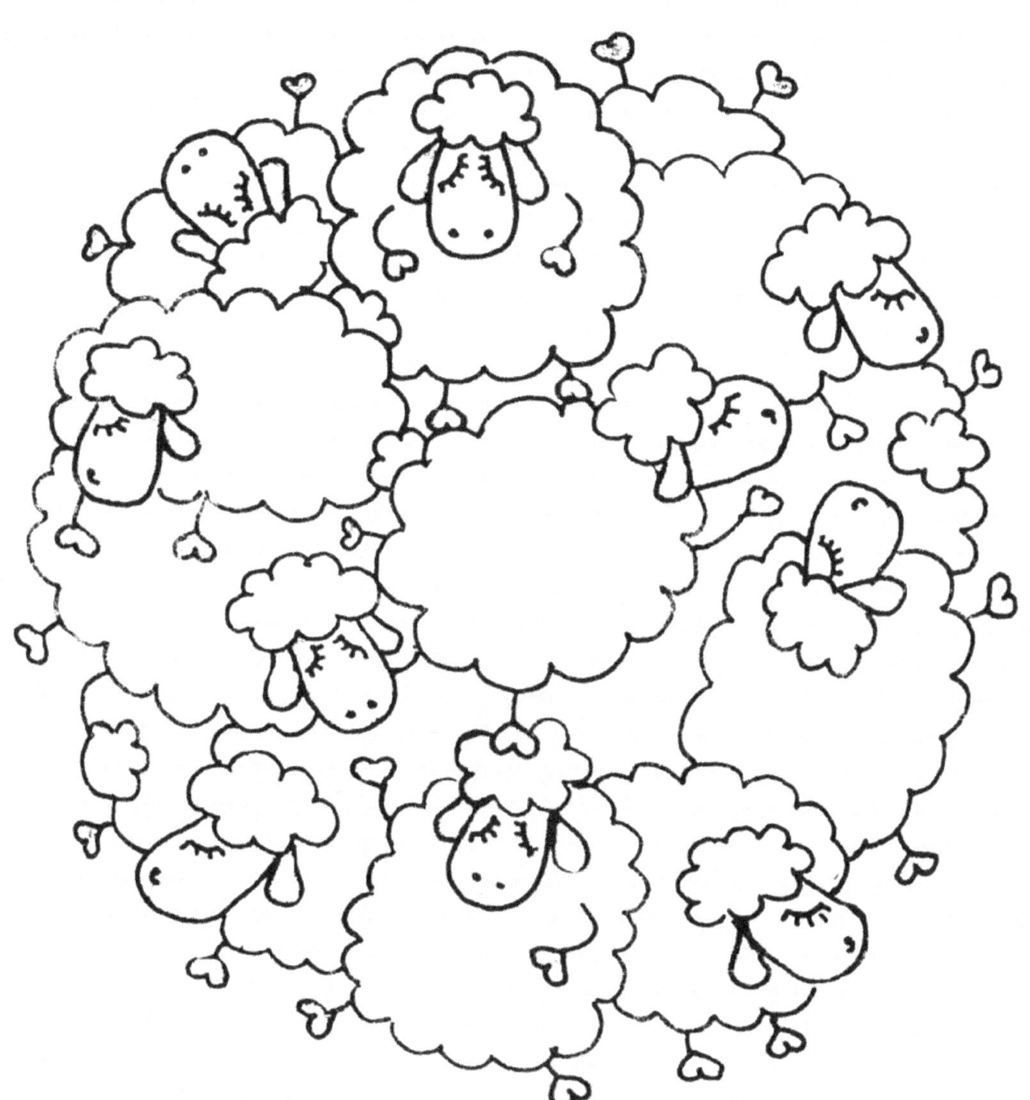

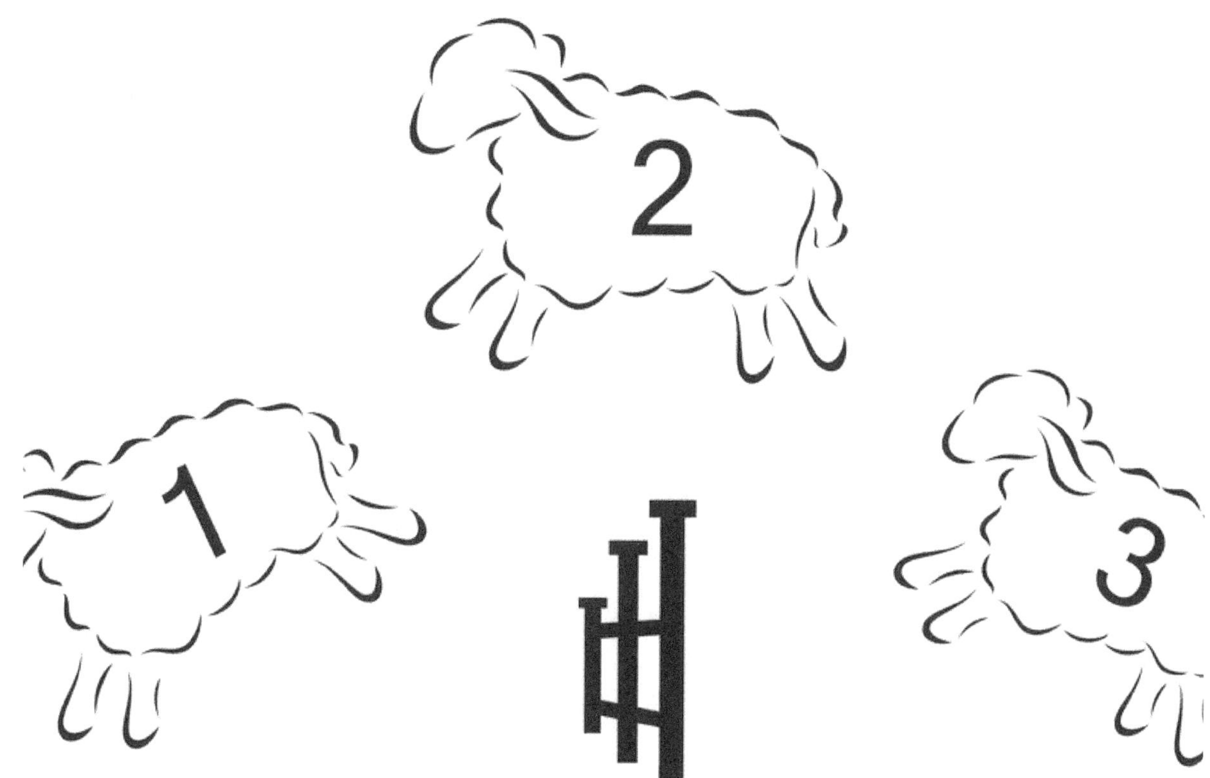
2
1
3

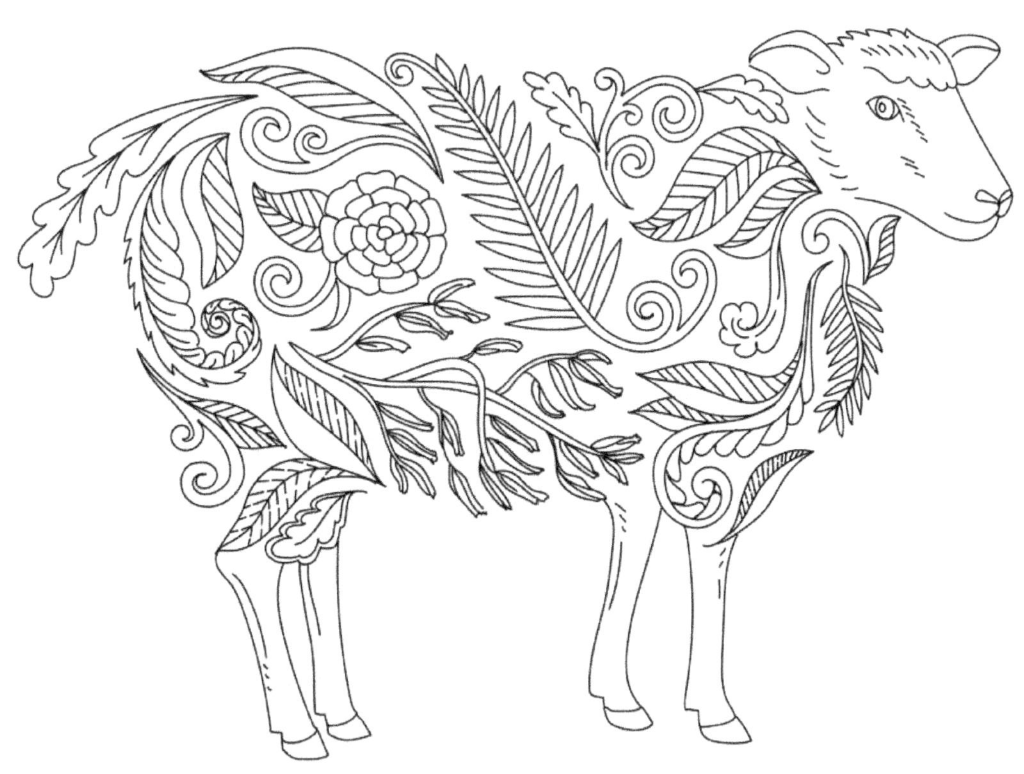

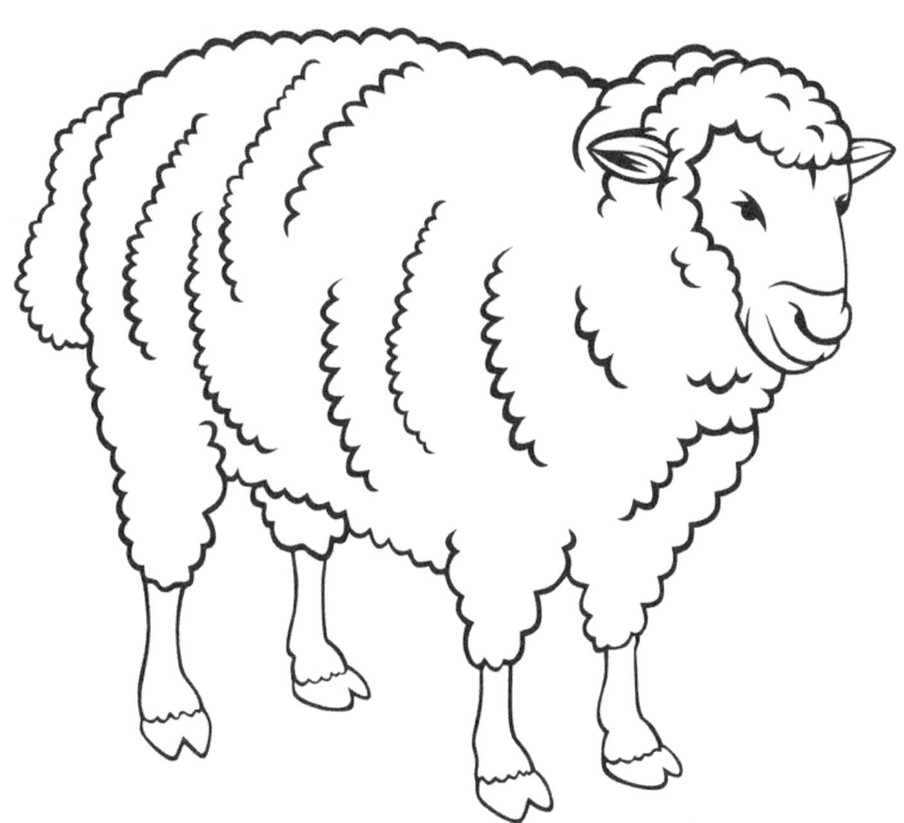

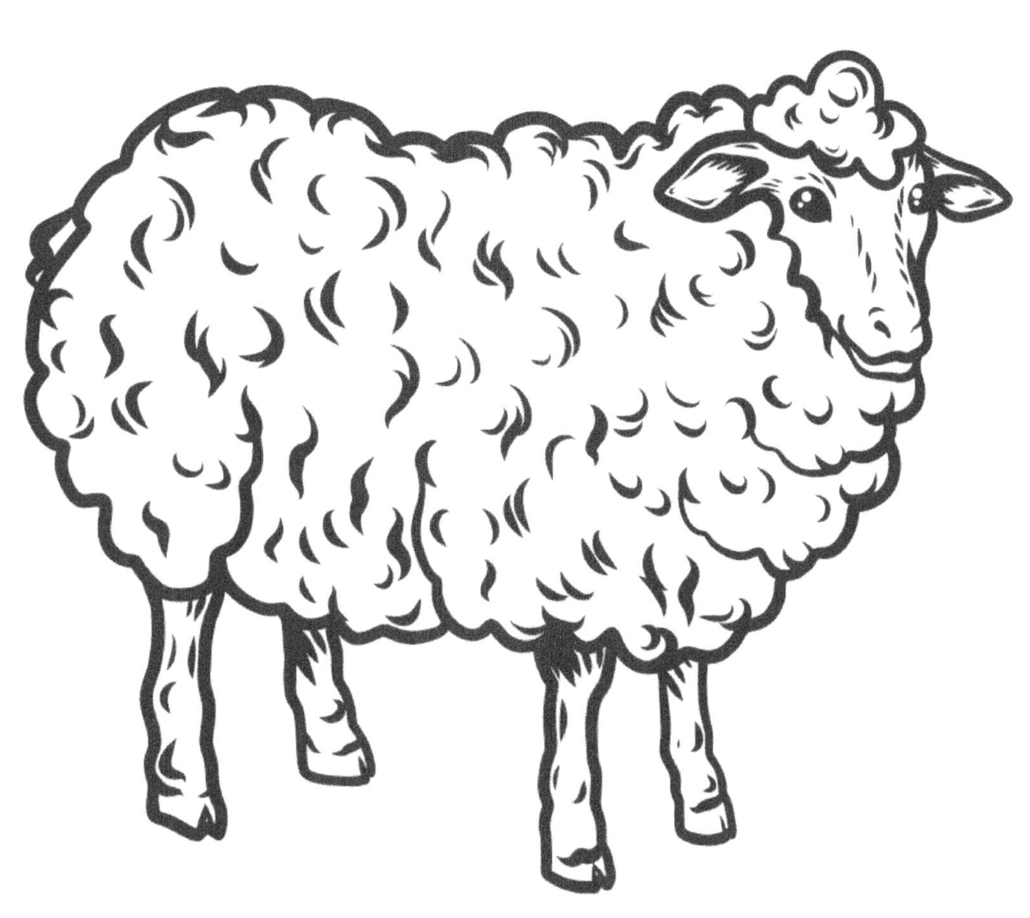

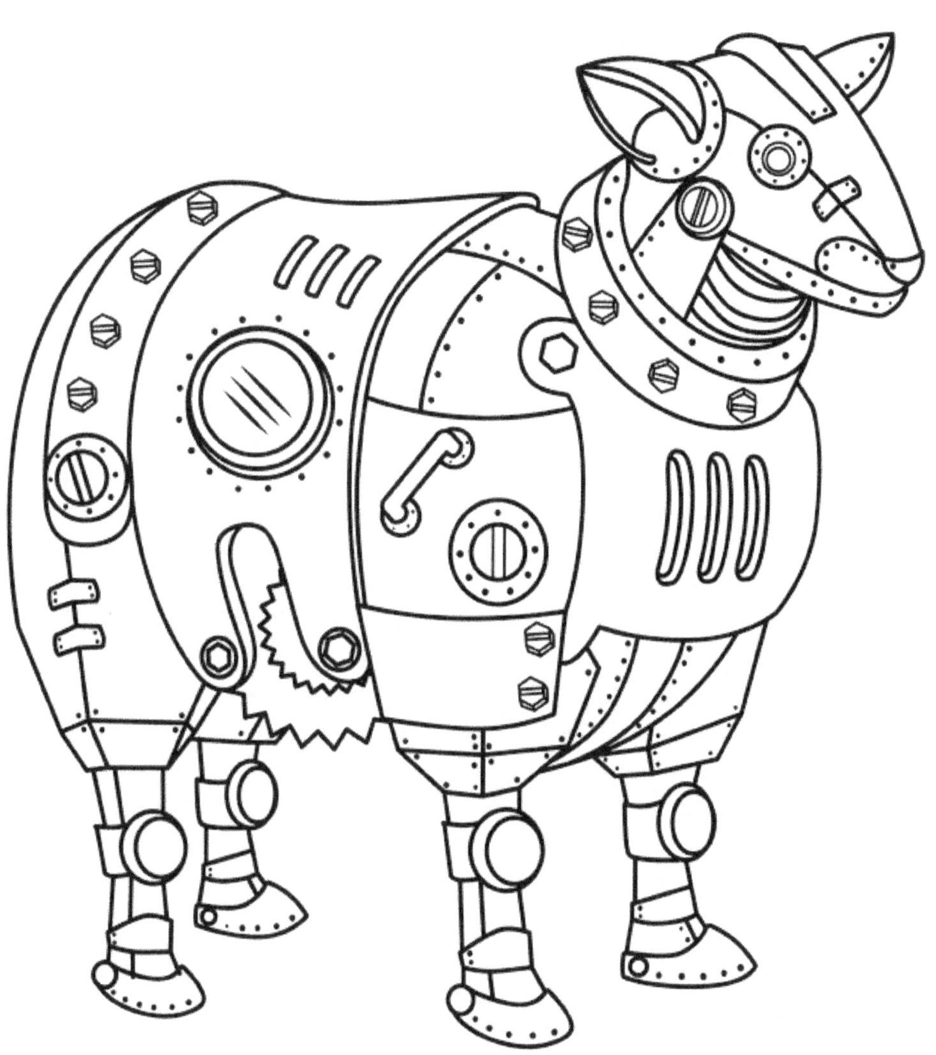

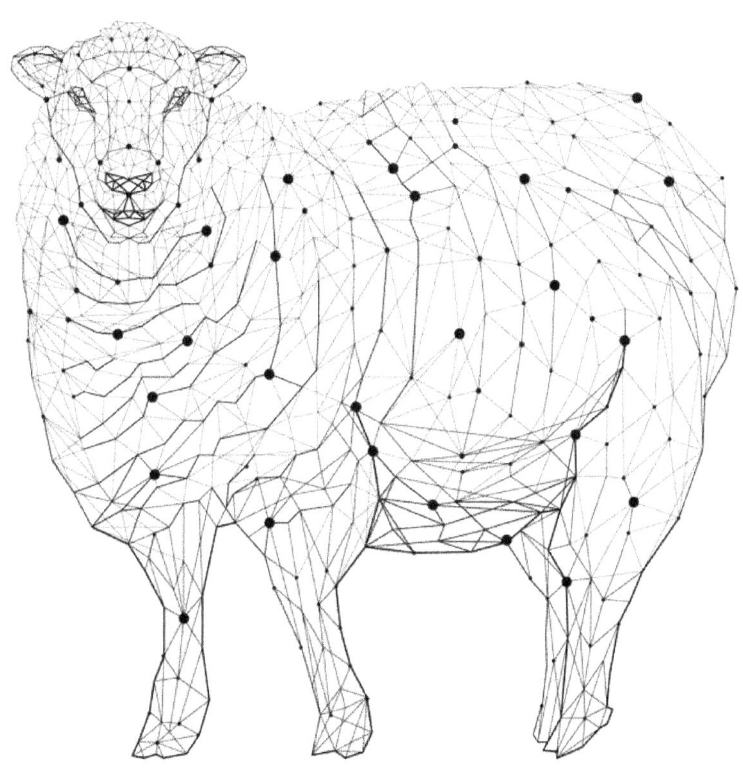

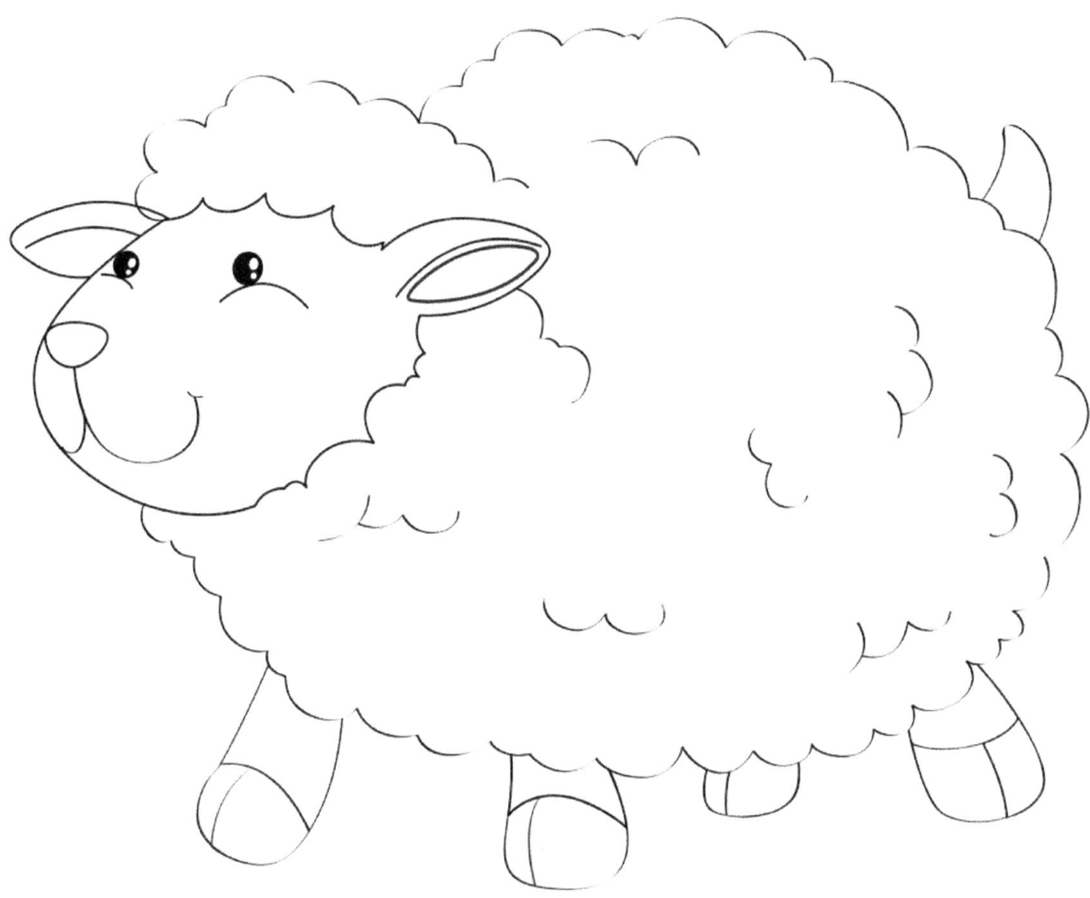

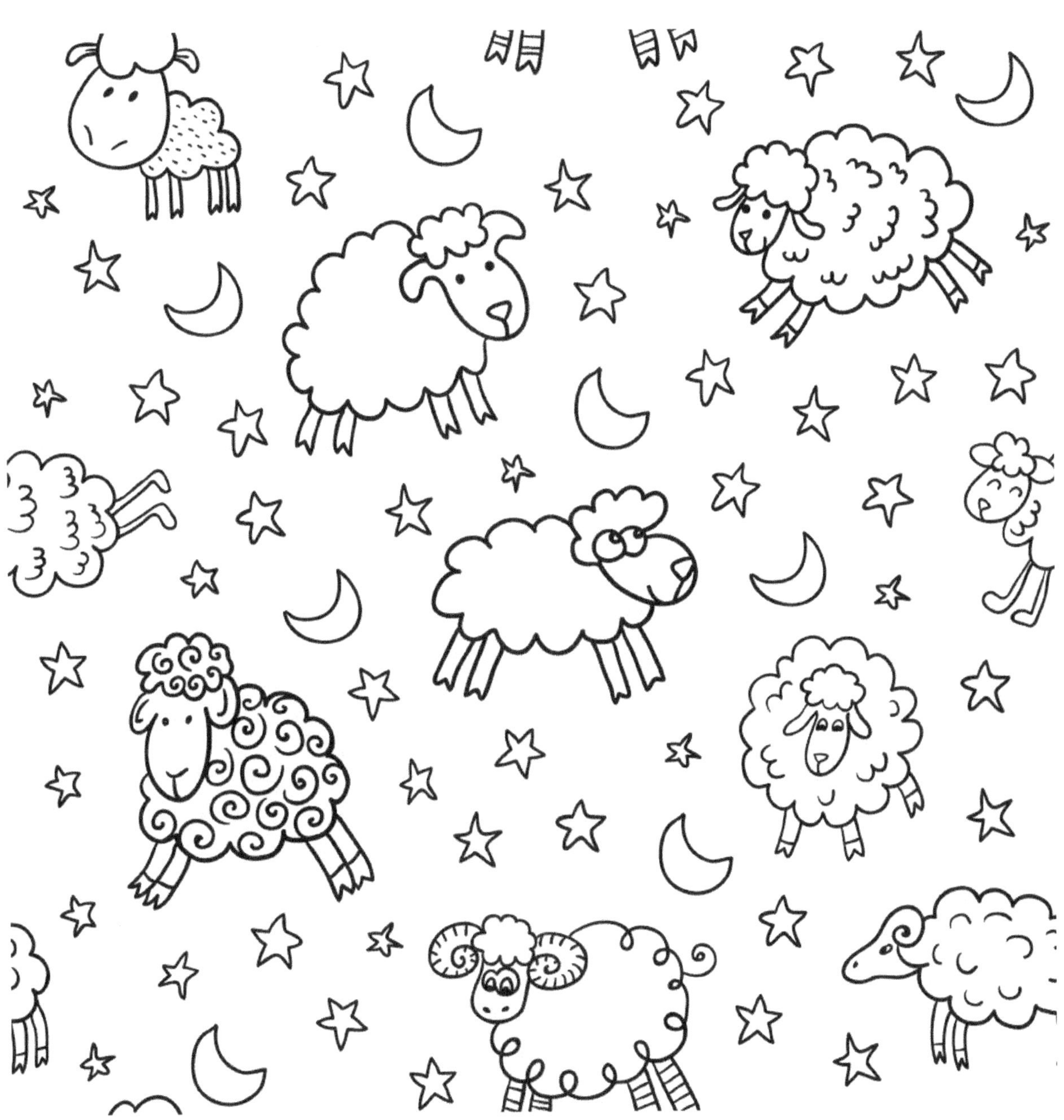